W9-CWU-597

ANIMAL BABIES

BABY LLAMAS

by Spencer Brinker

Consultant: Beth Gambro
Reading Specialist, Yorkville, Illinois

BEARPORT
PUBLISHING

Minneapolis, Minnesota

Teaching Tips

Before Reading

- Briefly discuss animal life cycles. Babies are born, they grow, and they have their own babies.
- Look through the glossary together. Read and discuss the words.
- Go on a picture walk, looking through the pictures to discuss vocabulary and make predictions about the text.

During Reading

- Encourage readers to point to each word as it is read. Stop occasionally to ask readers to point to a specific word in the text.
- If a reader encounters an unknown word, ask them to look at the rest of the page. Are there any clues to help them understand?

After Reading

- Check for understanding.
  - ▸ What are some things baby llamas do during the first few weeks? What about after that?
  - ▸ Why do people try and stay away from baby llamas?
  - ▸ Look at page 22. What did you learn about baby llamas from reading this book?
- Ask the readers to think deeper.
  - ▸ Other than size, what is one thing that is different about baby llamas and adult llamas?
  - ▸ What is one thing that is similar about baby and adult llamas?

Credits:
Cover, © ernstboese/iStock; 3, © DmitriyBurlakov/iStock; 4-5, © Masr/Dreamstime; 4-5, © CorbierePhotos/Shutterstock; 6-7, © meunierd/Shutterstock; 8-9, © ernstboese/iStock; 9, © John Lawson, Belhaven/Getty; 10-11, © kakemi/Shutterstock; 12, © JRLPhotographer/iStock; 13, © © mihtiander/iStock; 14-15, © Sergdid/iStock; 17, © Bill Miller/Alamy Stock Photo; 18-19, © Joshua Rainey Photography/Shutterstock; 20-21, © Cezary Wojtkowski/Shutterstock; 22, © Amy Johansson/Shutterstock; 23TL, © Karel Gallas/Shutterstock; 23TR, © Fraukje Vonk Photography/Shutterstock; 23BL, © JRLPhotographer/iStock; and 23BR, © mmac72/iStock.

Library of Congress Cataloging-in-Publication Data

Names: Brinker, Spencer, author.
Title: Baby llamas / by Spencer Brinker.
Description: Bearcub books edition. | Minneapolis, Minnesota : Bearport
  Publishing Company, [2021] | Series: Animal babies | Includes
  bibliographical references and index.
Identifiers: LCCN 2020015889 (print) | LCCN 2020015890 (ebook) | ISBN
  9781642809596 (library binding) | ISBN 9781642809664 (paperback) | ISBN
  9781642809732 (ebook)
Subjects: LCSH: Llamas—Infancy—Juvenile literature.
Classification: LCC SF401.L6 B75 2021 (print) | LCC SF401. L6 (ebook) |
  DDC 636.2/966—dc23
LC record available at https://lccn.loc.gov/2020015889
LC ebook record available at https://lccn.loc. gov/2020015890

Copyright © 2021 Bearport Publishing Company. All rights reserved. No part of this publication may be reproduced in whole or in part, stored in any retrieval system, or transmitted in any form or by any means, electronic, mechanical, photocopying, recording, or otherwise, without written permission from the publisher.

For more information, write to Bearport Publishing, 5357 Penn Avenue South, Minneapolis, MN 55419.

Printed in the United States of America.

Contents

It's a Baby Llama! 4

The Baby's Body 22

Glossary 23

Index 24

Read More 24

Learn More Online. 24

About the Author 24

It's a Baby Llama!

Llamas stand around a new baby.

The little baby cria is so cute!

Now, the **herd** has one more llama.

Say cria as KREE-uh.

5

Some animals lick their new babies.

But a llama mother does not.

Her tongue is too short!

This mother lies with the baby.

A llama can stand up about one hour after it is born.

It drinks milk from its mother's body.

The baby is about as heavy as a child that is two years old.

9

The cria hears with long ears shaped like bananas.

It looks with big eyes.

Soon, the baby is walking.

Llama feet have two toes.

Each toe has a big **nail**.

Nail

Most llamas live on farms or in zoos.

But people try to stay away from baby llamas.

The baby needs to **bond** with other llamas.

Llama babies drink milk for about six months.

Then, they eat grass and other plants.

A special **stomach** breaks down all the plants.

Llama poop does not smell!

It can be used to help plants grow.

The poop is sometimes called llama beans.

Can you see why?

Llamas do not need their mother's help after one year.

Soon, they can start having their own babies!

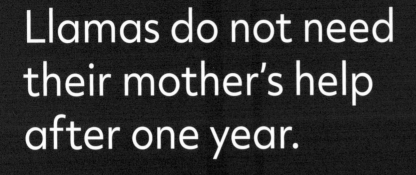

The Baby's Body

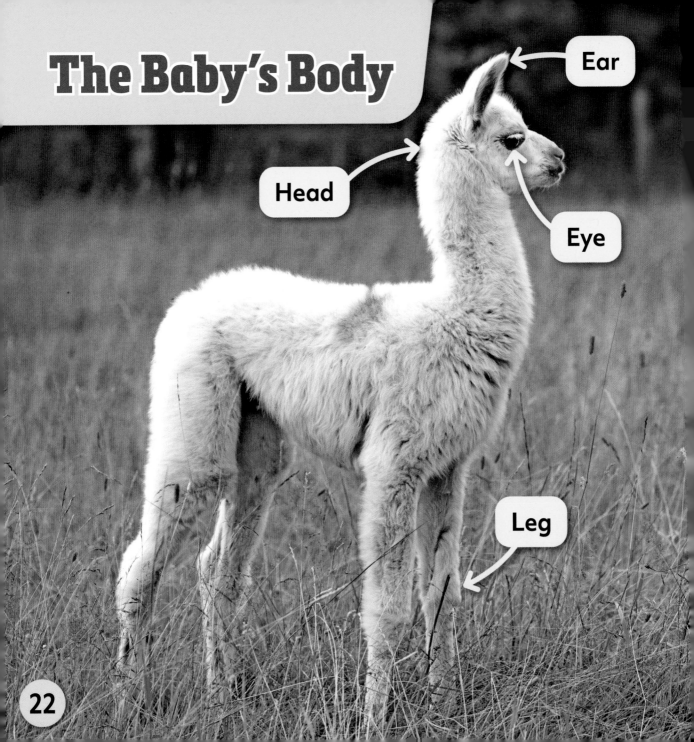

Ear

Head

Eye

Leg

Glossary

bond to form a close connection with

herd a group of animals

nail the hard covering at the end of a finger or toe

stomach the part of the body where food goes after it has been swallowed

Index

ears 11, 22		**milk** 8, 16	
eyes 11, 22		**mother** 6, 8, 20	
feet 12		**nails** 12	
herd 4		**plants** 16, 18	

Read More

Buller, Laura. *Llamas (DK Readers Level 2).* New York: DK Publishing (2019).

Leaf, Christina. *Llama or Alpaca? (Blastoff! Readers: Spotting Differences).* Minneapolis: Bellwether Media (2020).

Learn More Online

1. Go to **www.factsurfer.com**
2. Enter "**Baby Llamas**" into the search box.
3. Click on the cover of this book to see a list of websites.

About the Author

Spencer Brinker loves to tell "dad jokes" and play word games with his twin girls.